To Al

Blessings & Joy

[handwritten signature]

Dec 2008

GODLY LOVE

GODLY LOVE

A ROSE PLANTED IN THE
DESERT OF OUR HEARTS

Stephen G. Post

FOREWORD BY
Dr. Robert H. Schuller

TEMPLETON FOUNDATION PRESS
WEST CONSHOHOCKEN, PENNSYLVANIA

Templeton Foundation Press
300 Conshohocken State Road, Suite 670
West Conshohocken, PA 19428
www.templetonpress.org

© 2008 by Stephen G. Post

All rights reserved. No part of this book may be used or reproduced,
stored in a retrieval system, or transmitted in any form or by any means,
electronic, mechanical, photocopying, recording, or otherwise, without
the written permission of Templeton Foundation Press.

*Templeton Foundation Press helps intellectual leaders and others learn about
science research on aspects of realities, invisible and intangible. Spiritual realities include unlimited love, accelerating creativity, worship, and the benefits of
purpose in persons and in the cosmos.*

Designed and typeset by Gopa and Ted2, Inc.

Library of Congress Cataloging-in-Publication Data

Post, Stephen Garrard, 1951–
Godly love : a rose planted in the desert of our
hearts / Stephen G. Post.
p. cm.
Includes bibliographical references.
ISBN-13: 978-1-59947-151-8 (alk. paper)
ISBN-10: 1-59947-151-5 (alk. paper)
1. God—Love. I. Title.
BT140.P67 2008
231'.6—dc22
2008017961

Printed in the United States of America

08 09 10   11   12 13   10 9 8 7 6 5 4 3 2 1

To Sir John Templeton, who had such faith
and hope in a love that never fails.
The whole world is grateful.

There is a beautiful message in the book of Isaiah, chapter 35, verse 1, and part of that verse reads, "The desert shall rejoice and blossom like a rose." This idea has grounded my ministry in times of highest joy and deepest pain, suffering, and sorrow. . . . When you are in a desert, plant a rose. Plant a rose of liberation. Plant a rose of peace, a rose of reconciliation, and a rose of faith, hope, and love. And the desert will blossom.

—PASTOR OTIS MOSS JR., PREFACE TO
WHY GOOD THINGS HAPPEN
TO GOOD PEOPLE

CONTENTS

FOREWORD

O F ALL THE books on love that I have been exposed to in my lifetime, I have never read a single one so profound, so intelligent, and so concise in economy of words. That matches the superlative quality of this book.

If people have been reading the greatest books on love they cannot consider themselves widely informed unless they read this stunning summary by a man who comes from a respected background in theology, psychology, sociology, and science. Stephen Post is a renaissance man whom I admire profoundly. This is a book that will become the classic statement on what we in the Christian tradition know as agape love, revealed completely in the life of Christ.

Anyone who has heard Stephen Post speak on the topic of love, or who has spent a little time with him in quiet conversation, walks away with a sense of his depth and passion. He has devoted decades to this topic, and all of his accomplishments as a person of faith derive from his desire to understand here on earth the one thing that means the most in eternity—love. This book tells the story of his enriching relationships with M. Scott Peck, the great blues guitarist Reverend Gary Davis, the visionary philanthropist Sir John Templeton, Dame Cicely Saunders, and so many others who have enriched his life since youth.

Stephen Post founded the Institute for Research on Unlimited Love (www.unlimited-loveinstitute.com) with the support of Sir John Templeton in 2001. It is now considered the premier research program in the world focusing on research into the ways in which the spiritual experience of agape love can shape and transform our lives in wondrous ways. From *20/20* to Michael Feldman's *Whad'Ya Know*, from *Talk of the Nation* to the *New York Times*, from *The Hour of Power* to the United States Congressional Retreat, the work of his Institute has become known nationally and internationally. Few people have been able to creatively engage the popular culture so successfully with the ways and power of love.

This book is written in such an inspirational way that it will change lives for years to come. It will bring immense benefit to all who read it.

Dr. Robert H. Schuller
Founding Pastor
Crystal Cathedral

GODLY LOVE

Love never fails.

—ST. PAUL,
LETTER TO THE CORINTHIANS

Introduction

YEARS AGO I visited a nursing home in Chardin, Ohio, and sat down with a man named Jim. He was deeply forgetful, having lost his grasp on the connection between past and present as a result of dementia. He could not respond to any of my questions about his two sons, although I looked him in the eye and called him by name as an expression of respect. But Jim had a twig that he placed in my hands, and when he did so he smiled with tremendous warmth and joy. If love were electric, the room would have been on fire. Jim struggled to get out just three words—the only three

When days grow dark and nights grow dreary, we can be thankful that our God combines in his nature a creative synthesis of love and justice which will lead us through life's dark valleys and into sunlit paths of hope and fulfillment.

—MARTIN LUTHER KING JR.,
THE STRENGTH TO LOVE

words he spoke that morning—"God is love." I was amazed, but I knew that people in his condition have good days and bad days; they are capable of some rare coherence on a good morning after a deep sleep.

I asked the nurse about Jim's twig. It turns out that when Jim was growing up on an Ohio farm, his father—a devout Christian—loved him very deeply and treated him with great tenderness. Jim's father gave the boy a chore every morning—to bring kindling in for the fireplaces. Like so many of those with Alzheimer's, Jim had traveled back into his past and landed at the place where he felt most comforted, in the safe haven of love. For him, that twig symbolized the love of his father and the joy that Jim felt in doing a small, helpful chore early in life. I believe that for Jim it also symbolized Godly love. There, in the desert of deep forgetfulness, Jim was coping with the chaos of the present by clinging to emotional memories that conjured up the power of love. We all have a yearning for Godly love. The embrace of Godly love is so powerful that, in Jim's case, even the ravages of Alzheimer's could not break it.

An Inspiration

I met Jim in 1988, and he inspired me to spend the next twelve years of my life doing research and writing about the power of love and spirituality in the lives of the deeply forgetful and their caregivers. When he handed me his twig, he ignited a fire of curiosity in my heart and my mind.

Godly love is the one thing in this universe that is fully reliable and worthy of our deepest trust, no matter how much hardship or heartache enters our lives. We encounter disappointment and loss in our fleeting lives, times of exhaustion when we have no love of our own to give, either to others or to ourselves. It is in these deserts that Godly love can plant a rose in our hearts. As it is written in Isaiah 35:1, "The desert shall rejoice and blossom."

At times in life we feel only the destructive emotions of hostility, bitterness, and despair. The desert has burned us out, and we can offer water to no one, not even ourselves. We feel that our very existence rests on some meaningless cosmic mistake, and we lose all sense of purpose. In the desert, everyday people who were once joyful retaliate against the gift of life in a downward spiral of rage or, at the other end of the spectrum, cool indifference to their fate and the fate of others. This sense of "nothingness" does not subside with the accumulation of wealth, or with yet another moment of hedonistic pleasure that begins to feel old, although such novelties may temporarily distract us from our nihilism. Even the seasoned mystic has a dark night of the soul.

We love because he first loved us.

—1 JOHN 4:19

Come, my friends, 'tis not too late
to seek a newer world.

—ALFRED LORD TENNYSON

W. H. Auden's Experience

Then something happens, a sort of sweeping feeling of comfort through a connection with Godly love. Living religions, it has been said, contain a tension-in-unity among the intellectual, the institutional, the emotional, and the mystical. The quiet sense of Godly love as an ever-present reality evokes the emotional and the mystical. Our perception of Godly love need not be dramatic, or involve loud prayerful shouts that raise the roof. In these moments we have a mystical sense that the love we are feeling for ourselves and for others is far above our natural capacities. The poet W. H. Auden described his quiet experience of Godly love as follows:

> One fine summer night in June 1933 I was sitting on a lawn after dinner with three colleagues, two women and one man.

We liked each other well enough but we were certainly not intimate friends, nor had any one of us a sexual interest in another. Incidentally, we had not drunk any alcohol. We were talking casually about everyday matters when, quite suddenly and unexpectedly, something happened. I felt myself invaded by a power which, though I consented to it, was irresistible and certainly not mine. For the first time in my life I knew exactly—because, thanks to the power, I was doing it—what it means to love one's neighbor as oneself. I was also certain, though the conversation continued to be perfectly ordinary, that my three colleagues were having the same experience. (In the case of one of them, I was able later to confirm this.) My personal feelings towards them were unchanged—they were still colleagues, not intimate friends—but I felt their existence as themselves to be of infinite value and rejoiced in it.

I recalled with shame the many occasions on which I had been spiteful, snobbish, selfish, but the immediate joy was greater than the shame, for I knew that, so long as I was possessed by this spirit, it would be literally impossible for me deliberately to injure another human being. I also knew that the power would, of course, be withdrawn sooner or later and that, when it did, my greed and self-regard would return. The experience lasted in its full intensity for about two hours when we said good-night to each other and went to bed. When I awoke the next morning, it was still present, though weaker, and it did not vanish completely for two days or so . . .

At another time I saw the great love of God, and was filled with admiration at the infiniteness of it.

—GEORGE FOX, *A JOURNAL*

Auden captures an experience that is subtle and deeply emotional—Godly love that animates and enlivens his sense of awe for the gift of others.

Transcendent Moments

I have not had any mystical experience of Cosmic Consciousness, a dramatic experience of Oneness with the Universe, where love is all and all is love, and the boundaries of the self disappear. I am too much of a rationalist for such things to happen to me. But I *have* had transcendent moments like Auden's over the years from early adolescence through adulthood, and thus I have never doubted the reality of Godly love. Hope is to be open to surprise. We are given surprise experiences of Godly love that are a declaration of Ultimate Reality. Gone are all the destructive emotions, from hostility to indifference, and all the pointless strife and quarrels. "By contrast," reads Galatians 5, "the fruit of the Spirit is love, joy, peace, patience, kindness, generosity, faithfulness, gentleness, and self-control."

Some have said that God is dead. I say that God is not dead, but without Godly love, we are. We all deal with the stress of life, and we all have times when we feel more or less imperiled. We all try to maintain a positive outlook on life, especially when we are hurting. We all strive to transform through love the vengefulness and callousness that threaten to overwhelm our capacity for forgiveness and compassion. Yet we need something more powerful than our human capacities to free us from the negative emotions that rob our lives of meaning and hope. This is where metaphysics comes in; the experience of a numinous Unlimited Love that fills the universe is widely reported by countless everyday mystics. But outside of personal experience, we know virtually nothing about this Godly love.

Each one of us has the ordinary human capacity for unselfish, unconditional love, which is actually quite extraordinary. From one perspective, this capacity could be viewed as a miracle of creative evolution. Human dignity is grounded in Godly love much more than in reason alone. But our natural love pales in comparison to the nobility and spiritual majesty of Godly love, which infuses with divinity our more limited natural gifts in the earthy realm. In this sense, grace perfects and completes nature.

Faith in Love

It would be easy to lose hope in the power of love, but for faith. Faith that, in the sweeping drama of history, God, the Master Playwright, set the universe in motion and orchestrated human progress so that love would triumph in the end. This despite startling scenes of

I pray that our Heavenly Father may assuage the anguish of your bereavement, and leave you only the cherished memory of the loved and the lost, and the solemn pride that must be yours, to have laid so costly a sacrifice upon the altar of Freedom.

—ABRAHAM LINCOLN,
LETTER TO MRS. LYDIA BIXBY

immense cruelty and horrendous violence in which evil fills the stage. Thus, St. Paul linked faith, hope, and love in a divine twining. Without faith and hope, love does not illuminate our hearts in the darkness. Faith declares that despite all the cruel tyrants and wanton abusers of life, Godly love has already triumphed. Hatreds and greedy passions can rule for a while, but they never win the day.

It is better not to have lived than not to have loved. Godly love is always creative and never destructive; it is about growth and flourishing in those we love, including ourselves, and it is also about accepting people as they are. When the happiness and well-being of another person becomes as important to us as our own happiness and well-being—or even more so—love is present. All spiritual and ethical progress turns on the development of loving emotions, attitudes, and behaviors.

The assertion that Muslims do not know Divine Love is as absurd as claiming that Muslims know nothing of Divine Compassion. Neither Judaism nor Hinduism identifies God simply with love, but that does not mean either of these religions, any more than Islam, is devoid of the notion of Divine Love, which flowered for them in the Hasidic and *bhakti* movements, respectively.

—SEYYED HOSSEIN NASR,
THE HEART OF ISLAM

1. GODLY LOVE
AND HUMAN HATREDS

N MARCH 2007 I had the honor of spending several days north of Paris with the great Jean Vanier, then in his early eighties. Jean had founded L'Arche ("The Ark") some four decades earlier, when he was inspired by an experience of Godly love to invite two men with cognitive developmental disabilities into his home. Over the years, L'Arche homes have flourished worldwide as volunteers dwell with the disabled in communities of faith, prayer, and Godly love. I had attended meals in L'Arche homes in Cleveland on a number of occasions, and I had heard the grace said

The ignorant say Love and God are different;
none know that Love and God are the same.
When they know that Love and God are
the same, they rest in God's love.
—TIRU-MULAR, HINDU BHAKTI POET

Men are not flattered by being shown that
there has been a difference of purpose
between the Almighty and them.
—ABRAHAM LINCOLN

before eating, the hymns sung, and the energy of love that was palpable in the lives of those caregivers and in the experience of those they cared for and lived with.

Jean struck me as one of the most loving, Godly, and humble men I had ever met. He spoke quietly and brilliantly, and he exuded an infectious sense of fun. On one Sunday evening there was a Catholic Mass in an old renovated chapel from the fourteenth century. About one hundred people had gathered there, mostly L'Arche volunteers and people with disabilities. I saw a volunteer wheel one older man named David up to the priest for communion. That night, at dinner, I asked Jean what he thought David had gotten from receiving communion, for David was probably the most severely disabled and agitated person I had encountered there. Jean said, "Whenever David receives communion, he becomes more peaceful, and that is the power of God's love.

Remember, Stephen, we do not know much about the mystery of God's love and presence." Jean's pure, enduring, and expansive love clearly encompassed such a severely disabled man, and counted him among God's blessed.

EVIL IN GOD'S NAME

When I encounter a man like Jean Vanier, I feel that we must all stop thinking of God as the epitome of awesome power and strength in the conventional sense. This convention may be partly true, but we need to set it aside; otherwise, we begin to think of God primarily in terms of might, and human arrogance propels us into thinking that because my God is stronger than your God, violence is justified in God's name. If we think about God in terms of power, then religions become tainted with human arrogance. Far too many prayerful people are carrying rifles in the spirit of pure hatred and pretending that their hatred is somehow divinely sanctioned. This amounts to shallow religiosity, which only causes pain and undermines Godly love. The Lord of power and might is first and foremost the author and giver of all good things, the Divine Entity who nourishes us in love and brings forth from us good works.

We need to stop thinking that our definitions of God are complete and that our knowledge of God's will is total. Our definitions, even if divinely inspired, are still products of the human mind, and we can never fully understand the Divine. Religious doctrines, if adhered to arrogantly, tend to separate us from one another and shatter the unifying spirit of Godly love that all spirituality seeks to cultivate. When religions place doctrine and force above love, they foment massive evil—from

Peace in the celestial city is the perfectly
ordered, perfectly harmonious fellowship
of those who enjoy God and enjoy
one another in God.

—AUGUSTINE

The man who foolishly does me wrong,
I will return to him the protection
of my ungrudging love.

—BUDDHA

torture to terror, from coercion to conflict. Religious wars exemplify human tribalism and arrogance, both of which bring out the worst in us.

Hatred, hostility, and revenge are such strong emotions that they can crush our fragile sense of Godly love. The pseudospirituality of hatred runs counter to all genuine spirituality, which is always an adventure in love, an expression of love's deepest desires.

COUNTERING HATRED WITH GODLY LOVE

The love of power can sometimes overwhelm the power of love, so we must remain humble and guard against this. No matter how little we know about God, we can still experience Godly love. Only by taking Godly love much more seriously than we do now—even inculcating a profound love for one another among ancient, sworn enemies—can we expect to head off a spiral of widespread destruction.

Most of religion and spirituality is rooted in healing emotions, grounded in love. We will never achieve sustained peace in the twenty-first century unless all religions live up to those intrinsic ideals of Godly love, applying those ideals to all of humankind without exception.

The world shows no signs of becoming any less religious; we as humans will always have a passion for Ultimate Truth that provides safe haven and emotional security in times of distress. Yet we will only have a human future if we infuse universal Godly love into the rituals that religions create, and express through our actions spiritual emotions such as forgiveness and compassion. If our religions fail to promote universal Godly love, violence will sweep us all away.

Promoting Harmony and Peace

Godly love alone can realign the world in harmony and peace. Too many kill in God's name, claiming that they alone know the destiny God intends for humankind. Our limited human knowledge of any divinely inspired destiny to be played out on the human stage belies this specious—and dangerous—claim.

Love is the source of our greatest happiness and security; therefore love is the Ultimate Good, the Supreme Good. Nothing else comes close, for love underlies the creative energy that propels us from birth to death. The withholding of love drives to destruction those deprived of love's nurturing, its compassion, and its life-giving blessings. This occurs most notably in critical developmental periods during childhood. And it holds just as true for a

It is this recognition of the law of love as the highest law of human life, and the clearly expressed guidance for conduct that follows from the Christian teaching on love, applied equally to enemies and those who hate, offend and curse us, that constitutes the peculiarity of Christ's teaching.

—LEO TOLSTOY, *THE LAW OF LOVE AND THE LAW OF VIOLENCE*

child in a nursery as it does for an older adult in a hospice.

Our religions, which offer models of righteous living, must put into practice their visions of Godly love, or they fail us all.

Trusting in Him, who can go with me,
and remain with you and be everywhere
for good, let us confidently hope
that all will yet be well.
To His care commending you, as I hope
in your prayers you will commend me,
I bid you an affectionate farewell.

—ABRAHAM LINCOLN, FAREWELL ADDRESS
AT SPRINGFIELD, ILLINOIS

2. Godly Love Is . . .

N August 2005 I was at the Chautauqua Institution in New York state, presenting a week of lectures on the interface among science, theology, and Godly love. My cell phone rang. It was the producer for Michael Feldman's NPR show *Whad'Ya Know?*, inviting me to be Michael's special guest in the Palace Theatre in downtown Cleveland on September 17, a Saturday morning. Michael was curious, he said, about my Institute for Research on Unlimited Love. I said yes, but without knowing anything about the show. In early September I decided to listen to *Whad'Ya Know?* and realized that Michael can be a little cutesy and mischievous. So on the evening of September 16 I went for one of my quiet Godly love walks along Ohio's Chagrin River, and I asked, "Lord, what is Michael Feldman going to ask me?" Well, it came to me that Michael would ask me something like, "Now, Dr. Post, Unlimited Love? What kind of love are we talking about here?" So I thought through an answer after making a call to my good friend William Grassie.

The next morning, sitting on the stage with four thousand people in the studio audience and millions listening in, Michael introduced me and asked, "Now, Dr. Post, what kind of love are we talking about here?" And I had an answer ready: "Michael, it's the kind of love that gets people down to New Orleans after Hurricane Katrina, the kind of love that makes our otherwise merely competent medical students real healers, the kind of love that God has for us all, and the kind of love that I think these people in the Palace Theatre have for you!" Everyone stood up and applauded, and Michael asked people all over America what their experience of this kind of love was like.

SEVEN CHARACTERISTICS OF GODLY LOVE

So what kind of love *are* we talking about? Unlimited Love is Godly love—one and the same. Let me try to describe its seven salient features, however imperfectly.

1. Godly love is *fiduciary*. This term, which has not previously been applied to Godly love, comes from the Latin word for *faith*. It describes relationships like those between a parent and a child, or a doctor and a patient—although Godly love is perfect, so all human-based analogies pale in comparison. Let us not pretend

Agape is the holy, unconditional love God gives us regardless of what we look like, how much money we have, how smart we are, and even regardless of how unloving our actions may sometimes be.

—SIR JOHN TEMPLETON,
PURE UNLIMITED LOVE

that we are God's equals in knowledge, power, and love. God is our guardian, always acting with human well-being in mind. Nothing is more important to God than we are. Fiduciary relationships are between a knowledgeable and beneficent protector and a beneficiary who is unequal in power, and who has reposed trust and confidence in that protector. We rely completely on God's fidelity and unwavering love—there for our human benefit, and without which we are devoid of direction and hope. In English common law, a fiduciary must show the highest standard of care, and is expected to be extremely loyal, with no other commitments that would interfere with this loyalty. Our deviations from the righteous path, even if they are hurtful to God, can never in any way weaken the solid bedrock of God's fiduciary love for us.

2. Godly love is *covenantal*. Godly love naturally elicits in us a desire to live a good, upstanding, and righteous life. When we backslide away from such standards, our conscience drives us away from God, and we succumb to inner chaos. This is self-inflicted. It isn't that Godly love disappears or is no longer available to us, or that God is punishing us; rather, we ourselves feel guilt over having strayed from the proper path and we therefore punish ourselves. Eventually, we express repentance, a kind of spiritual apology, and begin to approach God anew. And when we do, Godly love is there for us. We always bask in the protective light and warmth of Godly love, but its intensity reveals to us our selfishness and narcissism, and this makes us want to live a better life. While we may waver, Godly love does not, for it is perfectly loyal, fiduciary, giving, and forgiving.

3. Godly love is *unconditional.* In this fiduciary relationship, Godly love is always available to us, no matter how egregious our past misdeeds. The relationship is not one between equals, in which God expects us to have the vision and virtue to always use our free will for noble purposes. There is absolutely nothing we can do to destroy God's love for us. Godly love leads to either triumph or tragedy, depending on how we use our free will, but because Divine love is always there, it enables us to turn tragedy into triumph. Godly love promotes emotional and spiritual healing.

4. Godly love is *personal.* By *personal* I mean that God knows every detail of our lives. God hears all our words, knows all our thoughts and feelings, sees all we do, and knows us by name. Love is always personal. This sense of a personal relationship

Cosmic consciousness is a third form which
is as far above Self Consciousness as is
that above Simple Consciousness. . . .
The prime characteristic of cosmic
consciousness is, as its name implies,
a consciousness of the cosmos,
that is, of the life and order
of the universe.
—RICHARD MAURICE BUCKE, MD,
COSMIC CONSCIOUSNESS

with God may be a little frightening; after all, it implies a certain measure of accountability and responsibility. But it also means that God knows precisely what each of us needs—better, even, than we ourselves do. The personal aspect of Godly love makes it intimate and grounds it in reality, rather than being some abstract energy swirling through the universe that does not really know or care about us.

5. Godly love is *unlimited.* That is, it does not hold anything back. There is a totality, an all-encompassing, sweeping aspect to Divine love. It is not merely kindness or benevolence, which, however important, have their limitations. We can be kind and benevolent to people we do not love. The New Testament speaks of Divine love as "self-emptying." This limitless self-giving has no interior constraints in its warmth and light. When we feel deeply that the

A sense of the universe, a sense of the *all*,
the nostalgia which seizes us when
confronted by nature, beauty, music—
these seem to be an expectation and
awareness of a Great Presence.

—TEILHARD DE CHARDIN,
THE PHENOMENON OF MAN

happiness and security of someone else
means as much to us as our own happiness and security, we love, but human love
fades. Godly love is unlimited because it
endures with a constant intensity, like a
beacon in the darkness. And it is unlimited because it includes every person
without exception.

6. Godly love is *nonviolent.* Under certain
unusual instances, the only way we may
be able to halt the power of the most ven-
omous hatred is through self-defense or
defense of the vulnerable. Dietrich Bonhoeffer, for example, a Lutheran pastor
and theologian, reluctantly concluded
that the only loving thing to do in the
face of Adolf Hitler's campaign of mass
murder was to try to assassinate the dic-
tator. But like all people of Godly love,
Bonhoeffer worked very hard to resist
evil through nonviolent means. There is

Someday, after mastering the winds,
the waves, the tides and gravity, we shall
harness for God the energies of love,
and then, for a second time
in the history of the world,
man will have discovered fire.

—TEILHARD DE CHARDIN

such a thing as a justified war when the forces of evil threaten annihilation of the good and the innocent. But even in such extreme cases, we must retain a sense of compunction, for in a better world such violence would not be necessary, even as a last resort. I prefer the strategy of non-violent resistance, advocated and carried out by African-American thinkers like Howard Thurman, Benjamin Elijah Mays, and Martin Luther King Jr., to the pacifism of the Amish and the Mennonites. Why? Because the African-American tradition of *agape* love—also known as Godly love—is active and proactive against evil within the whole of society; it does not separate itself from the world. There are too many today who either do not take seriously the idea that God is love, or who distort the goals of that love by appealing to coercion, threats, and

Behold the miracle! Love has no awareness
of merit or demerit; it has no scale by
which its portion may be weighed
or measured. It does not seek
to balance giving and receiving.
Love loves; this is its nature.

—HOWARD THURMAN,
THE INWARD JOURNEY

patterns of wanton violence. Godly love is a greater power than violence, and it forgives rather than exacting vengeance.

7. Godly love is *noncoercive.* In Fyodor Dostoevsky's novel *The Brothers Karamazov,* the author refers to God's choice to curb the Divine's own power as the "miracle of restraint." Jesus, when he was tempted in the desert, was offered all worldly power and dominion, but he refused. No displays of omnipotence would achieve the response he hoped for. He also refused to take up the sword. He died in a radical act of self-giving that compels only by the power of love. As it is written, "For what will it profit them if they gain the whole world but forfeit their own life?" (Matthew 16:26).

God's love is given to us not because we
deserve it. In fact, most likely when
we need love the most is when we
are most unlovable. Worthiness
is not a prerequisite to receive
the benefit of God's
love or grace.

—SIR JOHN TEMPLETON,
PURE UNLIMITED LOVE

3. OUR HUMAN SIGNIFICANCE

N OCTOBER 1999 the Institute for Research on Unlimited Love was beginning to take shape through a conference convened in Cambridge, Massachusetts. Among the leading lights of Godly love whom I invited to speak about their lives was the remarkable Templeton Laureate, Dame Cicely Saunders, then eighty-three years of age and known all over the world as the creator and founder of the hospice movement. Indeed, she took the name *hospice* from the medieval notion of a safe place where wayfarers might spend the night. She

And what does the Lord require of you?
To act justly and to love mercy and to walk
humbly with your God.

—MICAH 6:8

Lord, I do not know what I ought to be
asking of you. You are the only One
who knows what I need. You love me
better than I know how to love myself.
O Father, give your child what
I do not know how to ask
for myself.

—FRANÇOIS FÉNELON,
MEDITATIONS ON THE HEART OF GOD

viewed dying as a journey, and a hospice as a safe haven where people could die in love and grace, and without a tube in every orifice.

Dame Cicely, who had flown in from St. Christopher's Hospice in London, began her plenary address by stating that her entire life's work was guided by God and by her experience of Divine love, even though the standard professional textbooks made no mention of this. Indeed, Christian bookstores in England sometimes have entire sections devoted to Dame Cicely, who gained nursing and medical degrees as credentials for a single task—to enable people who are dying to experience a sense of significance. No, they are not beyond "care" simply because they are dying, nor need they be warehoused in dehumanizing, highly technological settings as though a few machines could afford them a sense of self-worth.

A MODERN-DAY SAINT

Dame Cicely changed the world, and did so because she felt so deeply that God loves people who are dying and wants their final months to be opportunities to sense the significance of their lives. At the end of her talk, Dame Cicely said that God has never allowed her to retire, and that she still goes into St. Christopher's to change bedpans, to listen attentively and express love, and to do all the small chores of hospice life with great love. She died several years later, and across the globe virtually every news organization printed voluminous obituaries to a modern-day saint who gave significance even to those who could no longer be rescued from death. I was blessed to be able to correspond with Dame Cicely for a number of years.

What fundamental human need does Godly love respond to in all its different incarnations?

Godly love responds to the deepest of human needs—the need for *significance.* It reflects back to the beloved his or her significance, dignity, and even sacredness. In the stress and struggle of life, as William James concluded, "The deepest principle of human nature is the craving to be appreciated." The need for significance is sometimes distorted into a quest for fame or renown. This quest may ultimately be self-defeating, even ruinous, because it usually lacks a grounding in God, who alone provides the significance that we seek.

It is so sad when our words and actions make someone else feel insignificant or cause others harm. This is primarily the ploy of insecure people, who feel a need to put others down in a misguided effort to gain higher social status. Some people are such masters at manipulating others into feeling that they have little or no worth that the target of this kind of malevolent campaign may be driven to suicide. Every day

Experience tells us that Man's true life
is neither lived in the material tracts of the
body, nor in the higher altitudes of the
intellect, but in the warm world of the
affections. Till he is equipped with these
Man is not human. He reaches his full height
only when Love becomes to him the breath
of life, the energy of will, the summit
of desire. There at last lies all
happiness, and goodness,
and truth and divinity.
—HENRY DRUMMOND,
THE ASCENT OF MAN

we see people treated as nothing more than chattel, the victims of exploitation, tyrannical ambitions, and the sheer will to control.

GODLY LOVE CONFERS DIGNITY

Through the lens of Godly love, we see equal significance in every human being. We are loved by God—all of us—and therefore our significance is firmly established in the universe. We owe our lives not to some cosmic error, but to the benevolent hand of a loving God who cherishes all of us. Our highest human dignity comes from the love that is within us by nature, and bestowed on us by God. There is no higher significance than this. We become, as it were, co-Creators in Godly love. In all the experiences people have of Godly love, they seem to exude a sense of how amazingly precious and significant they feel, ensconced in the deeply personal love of God.

In such a case the Divine Love does not *substitute* itself for the natural—as if we had to throw away our silver to make room for gold. The natural loves are summoned to become modes of Charity while also remaining the natural loves they were.

—C. S. LEWIS, *THE FOUR LOVES*

4. THE GREATEST SPIRITUAL EMOTION

WHEN I WAS a boy growing up on Long Island, I had the opportunity to study the guitar with the Reverend Gary Davis, a blind minister who was a big part of the folk revival movement of the 1960s. Reverend Davis was among the most famous African-American blues and gospel guitarists and singers of his generation, with a career that started in Durham, North Carolina, in the 1930s. He later became an ordained Baptist minister.

An African-American
Influence

In the summers I would sit in his apartment in Jamaica, Queens, with his beloved dog at his feet and Mrs. Davis in the kitchen. Reverend Davis, always wearing thick, dark-green sunglasses, would listen to me play classic African-American spirituals and occasionally interject a word or two of constructive criticism. We talked a lot about agape love: At the time I was studying the writings of Howard Thurman and other African-American theologians and mystics of Godly love. Indeed, this was the topic of my sacred studies papers at St. Paul's School in New Hampshire, where I was inspired by my teacher, the Reverend John T. Walker, an African-American Episcopal priest who knew Thurman and Benjamin Elijah Mays and Martin Luther King Jr. personally. Reverend Walker soon became the dean of the National Cathedral in Washington, D.C.

One day, as I was playing "Amazing Grace," Reverend Davis interrupted me and said, "Stevie Boy, you ain't a bad player at all, but you got to stick with your theology. I hope you keep studying here on this earth the one thing that means the most in heaven, and that's the love of God, boy, the love of God. And it ain't a concept, but it's something that just sweeps over you, quiet like. It's all about your heart."

A few years later, I helped bring Reverend Davis—dog and all—out to Reed College by plane to play one of our big Saturday concerts in the spring of 1970. Reverend Davis died in 1973, having influenced a generation of musicians with his legendary performances at the Newport Folk Festival, and his uncanny ability, imbued with deep spirituality and humility, to teach the guitar to the next generation.

He showed in all things a sensitive and
warmly responsive humanness. The Christian
who wants to imitate his Master must learn
to do so not by imposing a crude and
violent control on his emotions (and in
most cases his efforts to do so will be
a failure) but by letting grace form
and develop his emotional life in
the service of charity.
—THOMAS MERTON,
LIFE AND HOLINESS

Later in my life, in the 1990s, I reconnected with the African-American tradition of agape love as a holy emotion through the remarkable Clevelander, Pastor Otis Moss Jr., a spiritual mentor for many wonderful people, including Oprah Winfrey. Just being in Pastor Moss's presence, you could sense his quiet emotional depth of heart. He was generous enough to join the advisory board of my fledgling institute.

The Reverends Davis, Walker, and Moss are three of the greatest African-American teachers of Godly love that anyone could ever encounter. I am blessed to have known all three. As they taught, Godly love is not some arid intellectual principle, but a state of the heart.

HARMONY WITH THE UNIVERSE

Our inner peace comes from being in harmony with the Supreme Love in the universe, as does our most fruitful work in the world. Nestled within this Godly love, we experience an emotional shift away from self and toward others. We gain an inner security that allows us to love beyond the usual human boundaries of tenderness. An overwhelming sense of freedom and joy suffuses this harmony with the universe that, once experienced, is seldom forgotten.

Godly love can elevate and enlighten us every day by enveloping us in a sudden and surprising wave of compassion, by sweeping us along a path of forgiveness, by resonating in an unexpected spark of loyalty, by giving us the creative energy to perform some small good for someone else. Such reactions are in stark contrast to those meltdown moments when we lose faith in our dreams and live in fear and trembling. In moments of turmoil, Godly love enables us to be patient, for these moments are tests and will eventually subside. Godly love can be most powerful when we are most in need.

For many of us, worship is about creating a

ritual world in which Godly love assumes its rightful, exalted place in the universe; in this world, we find inspiration to live our lives with love. When we acknowledge and experience Godly love, we can live the best lives possible, making the most of our time on earth and contributing to the overall wellspring of goodness in the world.

Making Us Flourish

Godly love places each of us in the proper juxtaposition to the universe, so that our emotions, volitions, creativity, relationships, and health all flourish. In this holism, every part of our being is centered on the energy of love.

Spirituality is a turning to God in earnest. It is renewal of faith, hope, joy, gratitude, and love. *Spirit* comes from the Latin word *spiritus,* or "breath"; without the breath of Godly love invigorating us, we die in the desert.

The whole value of a benevolent deed lies
in the love that inspires it.
—TALMUD: SUKKAH 49B

Upon the whole, I think it clearly manifest,
that all truly gracious affections do arise
from special and peculiar influences
of the Spirit . . .
—JONATHAN EDWARDS, *A TREATISE CONCERNING
RELIGIOUS AFFECTIONS*

Catholics speak of love as being "infused," and this is a useful word. An *infusion* involves placing plants, like tea leaves, in water or oil and steeping them to bring out their flavor. Our hearts are steeped in Godly love to bring out the power of our love, enhanced and permeated by the warmth of the Divine.

DIVINE LOVE AS METAPHOR

We can view the creation story in Genesis 1 as a metaphor for our own interior lives, the lives of our souls or hearts. Our souls, too, are often void, formless, plunged in darkness, and full of unrealized possibilities. Hovering over this darkness is the same Godly love that fosters love in the void. We pray that Godly love will prompt each of our souls to take creative action for the world's betterment, sanctifying, quickening, and bringing to fruition loving-kindness in everyone and everything we touch.

This transformational and sanctifying love is also a moral grace that makes possible deep love of one's neighbor. People we encounter may be destitute and crazed, or may seem unalterably averse to the creative power of Godly love. But they, too, like all of us, are the stuff God works with to inspire goodness in the world. So, ultimately, we should never allow hate for anyone to take root in our heart, despite the powerful urge for revenge when we have been wronged. We need to have reverence for even the most unformed human nature, for it is on that raw material that Godly love can make the greatest difference. This moral grace allows us to see every person, no matter how flawed, as significant and worthy of our concern, kindness, and respect. We always fall short of expressing perfect love, and yet no limits can be set on the moral or spiritual potential of anyone in this life.

Godly love surpasses any human emotion, even when we are at our best, because it operates at a different order of magnitude than human love. This does not mean that human love lacks authenticity or immense importance within the natural scheme of things, or that it is not the soil in which Godly love takes root. But human love is still on the human plane, a reflected image of Godly love; it pales in comparison to the overwhelming experience of pure Unlimited Love, which is the love of God. Yet it is the point of contact within us that allows Godly love to blossom in the world.

Nihilistic Naysayers

The great cynical minds, from Sigmund Freud to Jean-Paul Sartre, tell us that there is no Godly love in the universe, that we cannot be saved, and that even at our most compassionate there is no authentic love, no genuine car-

'Tis an evidence that true religion, or holiness
of heart, lies very much in the affection
of the heart, that the Scriptures place
the sin of the heart very much in
hardness of heart.

—JONATHAN EDWARDS, *A TREATISE CONCERNING
RELIGIOUS AFFECTIONS*

ing, within our hearts. Sartre asserted that any "look" of compassion is purely manipulative, and Freud inveighed against the very idea of neighborly love. Other lesser minds followed suit.

As a teenager, I saw Samuel Beckett's secular, existentialist play *Waiting for Godot* and came away feeling that the purpose of life was to look like Humphrey Bogart with dyspepsia. Such malaise gets us nowhere but deeper into the desert. Futility may prevail for a day, but for us to thrive we need to put our faith in life's deeper possibilities and embrace Godly love.

The time has come for humanity not only
to begin to understand the nature, forms,
and how and why of love, but also
to endeavor to design more efficient
techniques for its production.

—PITIRIM A. SOROKIN,
THE WAYS AND POWER OF LOVE

5. Five Dimensions of Godly Love

S A TEENAGER, I attended a talk in a church in Concord, Massachusetts, by a visiting lecturer, Harvard's Pitirim A. Sorokin (1889–1968), who founded the Harvard Center on Creative Altruism. Later, when I was a graduate student at the University of Chicago in the early 1980s, I was writing a PhD dissertation on agape love and the flourishing of those through whom it flows. At that point, I read Sorokin quite seriously. He has influenced me in the discussion of Godly love and science over the decades, especially because he effectively described such love along five axes. Godly love would be perfect in all of these dimensions, as Sorokin suggested in his classic work, *The Ways and Power of Love: Types, Factors, and Techniques of Moral Transformation* (Philadelphia: Templeton Foundation Press, 2002 [original 1954]). Sorokin's first dimension of love is *intensity*. Low-intensity love makes possible minor actions, such as giving a few pennies to the destitute or relinquishing a bus or train seat for another's comfort. By contrast, at high intensity, much that is of value to the person expressing that love (time, energy, resources) is freely given.

Sorokin's second dimension of love is *extensivity*: "The extensivity of love ranges from the zero point of love of oneself only, up to the love of all mankind, all living creatures, and the whole universe. Between the minimal and maximal degrees lies a vast scale of extensivities: love of one's own family, or a few friends, or love of the groups one belongs to—one's own clan, tribe, nationality, nation, religious, occupational, political, and other groups and associations" (16).

Sorokin next added the dimension of *duration,* which "may range from the shortest possible moment to years or throughout the whole life of an individual or of a group" (16). For example, the soldier who saves a comrade in a moment of heroism may then revert to selfishness, in contrast to the mother who cares for a sick child over many years. Romantic love, he notes, is generally of short duration as well.

The fourth dimension of love is *purity*. Here Sorokin wrote that our love is characterized as affection for another that is free of egoistic motivation. By contrast, pleasure, advantage, or profit underlie inferior forms of love, and these inferior forms of love will fade in short order. Pure love—that is, love that is truly disinterested and asks for nothing in return—represents the highest form of emotion (17).

Through God, in the strength of God, he loves all mankind with a divine love. This is not the fraternity enjoined on us by philosophers in the name of reason, on the principle that all men share by birth in one rational essence: so noble an ideal cannot but command our respect; we may strive to the best of our ability to put it into practice, if it be not too irksome for the individual and the community; we shall never attach ouselves to it passionately. Or, if we do, it will be because we have breathed in some nook or corner of our civilization the intoxicating fragrance left there by mysticism.

—HENRI BERGSON,
THE TWO SOURCES OF MORALITY AND RELIGION

Finally, Sorokin focused on the *adequacy* of love. Inadequate love is subjectively genuine but has adverse objective consequences. It is possible to pamper and spoil a child with love, or to love without practical wisdom. Adequate love achieves ennobling purposes and is, therefore, anything but blind or unwise. Successful love cultivates the building of character and virtue, and shuns overindulgence.

MEASURING LOVE

These five dimensions of love allow us to ask empirical questions about how strength or weakness in one dimension varies across other dimensions. How intense, extensive, enduring, unselfish, and wise is any particular manifestation of love? Sorokin argued that the greatest lives of love and altruism approximate or achieve "the highest possible place, denoted by 100 in all five dimensions" (19), while per-

How could love be rightly discussed if You
were forgotten, O God of Love, source
of all love in heaven and on earth,
You who spared nothing but gave all in love,
You who are love, so that one who loves
is what he is only by being in You!

—SØREN KIERKEGAARD,
WORKS OF LOVE

sons "neither loving nor hating would occupy a position near zero" (19). Gandhi's love, for example, was intensive, extensive, enduring, pure, and adequate (effective). Of special interest to Sorokin was the love of figures like Jesus, Al Hallaj, and Damien the Leper. Despite being persecuted and hated, and therefore without any apparent outside source of love energy to tap into, they were nevertheless able to express love at high levels in all five dimensions. Such love seems to transcend ordinary human limits, which suggested to Sorokin that some human beings do, through spiritual and religious practices, draw strength from a love energy that is the very definition of God.

Sorokin was convinced that such perfect love can best be explained by hypothesizing an inflow of love from a higher source whose beneficent power far exceeds that of human beings. Those who were despised and had no psychosocial inflow of love to sustain them must receive love from above:

The most probable hypothesis for them (and in a much slighter degree for a much larger group of smaller altruists and good neighbors) is that an inflow of love comes from an intangible, little-studied, possibly supraempirical source called "God," "the Godhead," "the Soul of the Universe," the "Heavenly Father," "Truth," and so on. Our growing knowledge of intra-atomic and cosmic ray energies has shown that the physico-chemical systems of energies are able to maintain themselves and replenish their systems for an indefinitely long time. If this is true of these "coarsest" energies, then the highest energy of love is likely to have this "self-replenishing" property to a still higher degree. We know next to nothing about the properties of love energy. (26)

Grace from Above

In Sorokin's view, people of great love who sustained love in the face of terrible adversity are graced. Those who are strong in all five aspects of love reflect, he conjectured, a divine love energy.

On a scale of one to ten on each aspect of love, most of us would rate ourselves relatively low. If Godly love is a perfect ten, I would rank Dame Cicely Saunders, who founded the hospice movement, an eight for her loyalty to the dying. I would rate Millard Fuller, who founded Habitat for Humanity, an eight for his loyalty to the homeless. But I would rank myself low, perhaps at about five, even though I consider loyalty a major personal strength of mine. Too

He is the Good, the unchangeable, overflow-
ing fountain of good that sends forth
nothing but good to all eternity. He is the
Love itself, the unmixed, unmeasurable Love,
doing nothing but from love,
giving nothing but gifts of love to everything
that He had made; requiring nothing
of all his creatures but the spirit and
fruits of that love which brought
them into being.

—WILLIAM LAW,
THE SPIRIT OF PRAYER

many times over the years my love has ebbed when it should have endured. Godly love never fades away.

So when we think of Godly love, we feel the gap between its perfection and our own imperfection. Sometimes we can only forgive ourselves because we know that God loves us so perfectly, and that we are therefore already forgiven by a power far greater than ourselves. Godly love inspires, but it also judges, drives us to repentance, and lures us to the path of greater holiness. Godly love is always a direction we follow, rather than a destination. And yet, some people come very close to it, but these individuals are rare indeed, and we call them saintly.

A word on extensivity. Whom should we love? Everyone? If so, can we ever succeed in this endeavor? Isn't love for everyone without exception" a realistic notion for God alone? The Greeks felt that love should be confined to those who are worthy of it. Aristotle argued that we should only love people as friends if they are virtuous. It might be acceptable to express occasional benevolence to others simply because they, too, are human beings, but this should be rare. In contrast to the Greeks, the Christian tradition urges full extensivity. As the seventeenth-century Anglican divine Jeremy Taylor wrote, "When friendships were the noblest things in the world, charity was little."

EVERYONE DESERVES LOVE

Where Christianity has guided our understanding of Godly love, love in its most profound form is not something another person earns. All of us, without exception, are worthy of one another's love simply because we are members of the human race. Ingroups tend to increase antagonism and conflict unless they are infused with some sense of brotherly or sisterly love that encompasses outsiders as well.

At some fundamental level, then, we either love everyone or we love no one. However, most thinkers in the Western tradition contend that universal benevolence is out of reach for all of us, and that for us to even approach this ideal, Godly love must enter our hearts. In this sense, Godly love alone can guide us toward universal loving-kindness and good-will toward all, and we humans can only exude such love by God's grace.

From Freud and his disciples down to the advocates of sociobiology, Western thought has discounted the possibility of universal human love. After all, how can we realistically feel a sense of deep, abiding love for the vast multitudes around the world with whom we have no ties and little in common? How can love be expected to blossom and thrive when our bonds with the "stranger" and the "neediest"

In the evening I went very unwillingly to
a society in Aldersgate-street, where one was
reading Luther's preface to the Epistle
to the Romans. About a quarter before nine,
while he was describing the change which
God works in the heart through faith
in Christ, I felt my heart
strangely warmed.

—JOHN WESLEY,
THE JOURNAL OF JOHN WESLEY

are relatively weak, even if we do feel a general sense of goodwill toward the human family?

Becoming Forces for Good

Here Godly love shows us the way, inspiring people to become forces for good for all people, with deep compassion and an abiding faith that our efforts will bring about a better world. The Quaker John Woolman and the slave trader John Newton were both moved by powerful experiences of Godly love to devote their lives to a love of all humanity, including the slaves. Like these great men, who found common ground within the embrace of Godly love, we, too, can truly love all humanity—both as a collective and as individuals—no matter how distant they are from us or how much they have failed to measure up to some ideal image we may hold of virtuous people.

The light that shines above the heavens
and above the world, the light that shines
in the highest world, beyond which
there are no others—that is the light
that shines in the hearts of men.

—FROM THE UPANISHADS

6. GODLY LOVE HOLISM

N AUGUST 2004 I was at a business meeting in New York City. It was a meeting that was leading nowhere, but I could not vote with my feet; I simply could not insult the people I was with. As 9:30 p.m. came and went, I had no chance of catching my flight from Newark to Cleveland. I had a lecture scheduled for 8 a.m. the next day, one that I couldn't miss. So I walked over to the Port Authority Bus Terminal on Eighth Avenue in the 100-degree heat and got on a bus. The driver turned around and said, "Sorry, folks. Air-conditioning's busted.

Do ya really wanna go to Cleveland?" We grudgingly consented.

About five minutes into the trip I felt a gentle tapping on my right shoulder. I turned around. There was a young fellow, perhaps eighteen or so, with the facial features of someone with Down syndrome. In a remarkably gentle, warm, and loving voice, he asked me, "Sir, are we in Cleveland yet?" I answered, "No, but I will be sure to let you know when we are, okay?" Well, every five minutes across New Jersey and Pennsylvania, along my favorite highway, Interstate 80, he asked me the same question and he got the same answer. We became friends in the process.

Now, talk about an emotional contrast! In the seat right in front of me was a guy with two little boys who might have been just five or six years old. About every half-hour this guy jumped up and slammed his fist into the metal ceiling of the bus, yelling an expletive and scaring everyone on board. We got to Milesburg, Pennsylvania, at about 4 a.m. Milesburg's one claim to fame is a 24/7 rest stop for buses. We all got out, bought snacks, freshened up, and headed back to the bus. But the security officer would not allow the fellow in front of me and his two boys back on the bus. As the bus pulled away, the irate passenger was kicking the side of the building, screaming, and his boys were in tears. We headed west on I-80, and almost immediately the kid behind me asked yet again, "Sir, are we in Cleveland yet?" Well, we arrived at the Cleveland Greyhound station on Chester Avenue at about 7 a.m., I gave the kid behind me a hug, met his family, and made it to my lecture on time.

So what is the point of this story? Simple. If you want to go to Cleveland, hostility won't get you there. It will get you marooned in Milesburg, Pennsylvania. But love will get you there, even if you are cognitively limited. Godly love

Those who refresh others will themselves
be refreshed.
—PROVERBS 11:25

'Tis better to give than to receive.
—ACTS 20:35

Perfect love casts out fear.
—1 JOHN 4:18

is the best way to ride the bus of life! And it turns out to be healthy, too.

In the first recorded exhortation of Godly love, Leviticus 19:18, we read, "You shall not take vengeance or bear a grudge against any of your people, but you shall love your neighbor as yourself." In this passage love—with all its warmth, compassion, and emotional depth—is juxtaposed with hostility and the spirit of revenge. Here we see that love casts out negative emotions, which need to be driven away because they don't leave easily on their own. Another passage in the Hebrew Bible, Proverbs 11:13, reads, "Those who refresh others will themselves be refreshed." We are refreshed not because we anticipate a reciprocal kindness, or a better reputation, but simply because we are engaged in the positive emotional energy of love, and it is within the sphere of love that we live best. To love is to be in harmony with oneself. I believe this is what St. Francis of

Assisi meant when he prayed, "For it is in giving that we receive." And it is what Plato meant when he said, famously, that virtue is its own reward.

Our Emotional Salvation

Godly love saves us from the abyss. If love sounds unappealing, consider the alternatives. Short-term anger may be necessary for self-preservation, but long-term negative emotional states destroy happiness and health, like acid slowly corroding metal. Our hearts just cannot take it. As cardiologist Redford Williams has shown, the most hostile among us have a 20 percent mortality rate by age fifty, and the least hostile have a mere 2–4 percent mortality rate. Even short-term anger is often misplaced or turns into a needlessly vicious rage; in the aftermath, we wish we had handled things with more dignity and restraint.

So how do we steer clear of unhealthy hatred—a rage for revenge against individuals who've done us wrong or the universe that has dealt us a difficult hand—and deadly indifference to the needs of others? The one answer that keeps recurring across the eons is to cultivate love. In the end, for the sake of others—but also for our own happiness and health—we can most fully and resiliently cope with the stress of a life by nurturing the emotional state of love, by keeping our hearts in the right place. Godly love helps us to do that, especially when we are on the verge of collapsing into bitterness and protracted rage, leading to a soul-stultifying depression.

Even though anger may make short-term sense as a response in certain situations, many people choose to forgo anger, condemnation, enmity, and any emotion rooted in ill will, especially as they get older. Leo Tolstoy, in his *Calendar of Wisdom*, wrote that anger gets

It is no measure of health to be well-adjusted
to a profoundly sick society.

— KRISHNAMURTI

When I do good, I feel good: when I do bad,
I feel bad, and that is my religion.

—ATTRIBUTED TO ABRAHAM LINCOLN

out of control much too easily. Godly love, as he experienced it, enabled him to live with a blessed sense of serenity, gratitude, love, forgiveness, awe, faith, and hope.

Of course, a little well-timed anger may be an important tool for reining in the excesses of harmful people, so it does have its uses. And yet St. Gregory listed it among the deadly sins: "The seven deadly sins are pride, lust, sloth, envy, anger, covetousness, and gluttony." Allowed to run wild, anger kills.

ABANDONING HATE; EMBRACING LOVE

Our whole being can be reordered and rightly organized by Godly love. As a result of embracing Godly love, countless people have done good in the world with renewed, even boundless, energy, despite adversity and setbacks.

Love, thou force of gravitation in the spiritual world, no individual life and no development is possible without thee!

—**FRIEDRICH SCHLEIERMACHER**

They are not disheartened; they do not lose faith. Rather, they abandon hate, anger, and fear, harmonizing their spiritual emotions with the universe and universal love.

To reject Godly love is to live a shallow, superficial life, devoid of deeper meaning and connection. The joyousness that comes from loving others is incompatible with contempt or indignation.

As my Father has loved me, so I have loved you; abide in my love. If you keep my commandments, you will abide in my love, just as I have kept my Father's commandments and abide in his love. I have said these things to you so that my joy may be in you, and that your joy may be complete. And this is my commandment, that you love one another as I have loved you.

—1 JOHN 15:9–12

7. GODLY LOVE AND HAPPINESS

I GREW UP WITH a very Irish mom, Molly Magee—well, in full, Marguerite Shea Magee. She met my dad in 1947 when he crashed into the rear end of her Chevy on the Long Island Expressway, and she was able to give him a ride home because his car was totaled. Without this little Godly coincidence, I would never have had the chance to get started!

When I was a young boy growing up in Babylon, Long Island, I had those occasional boring days that drove Mom nuts. She would always say to me, "Now, Stevie, instead of moping around, why don't you go out and do something for someone!" And I would. I used to help folks in the neighborhood rake leaves, pull boats out of the Great South Bay to dry-dock them, shovel snow, and do other helpful chores. These were small actions, the kind we all can do. What I noticed was that I always felt happy afterwards, and was smiling from ear to ear. So from about age ten I knew that happiness was often about doing for others. I was also a prayerful Roman Catholic, more so than anyone else in the family, and somehow love of God, love of one's neighbor, and love of self all meshed into one for me. Much of my research and writing over the years has followed Mom's teaching, from a PhD dissertation at the University of Chicago reconciling agape love with happiness, to recent books like *Altruism & Health* (Oxford University Press, 2007) or *Why Good Things Happen to Good People* (Broadway

Books, 2007), both explaining why it's good to be good.

The Roots of Happiness

Happiness is rooted in putting ourselves in the proper alignment with Godly love, with embracing that love, which is higher—more selfless, more all-encompassing—than our own. Those pursuing surface pleasures find that ultimate happiness eludes them, but those who know they are loved by God are able to craft meaningful lives in the service of God and their fellow people.

We seek our authentic selves, and we seek happiness. The two are essentially one. In the eudaemonist heritage that goes back to Aristotle, happiness means that we flourish over our entire lifetime. This vision is substantially different from hedonism and the drive to acquire ever more material things. So what makes us

The Holy Spirit rests only on him who
has a joyous heart.
—TALMUD, SUKKOT 5.1

How good it is to celebrate the spirit of God
within us by quiet acts of adoration and
praise; to remind ourselves of all the ways
by which His grace has watered the roots
of our being, giving to us manifold
strengths, creating miracle after miracle
in the midst of the common task and
the common way that we take.
—HOWARD THURMAN,
THE CENTERING MOMENT

flourish in a profoundly satisfying and soul-nourishing way? The Godly love that brings inner peace, enduring love, and rapturous hope to our lives.

Love alone lets us flourish over an entire lifetime, and when we live a life suffused with love, even the simple, hedonistic pleasures of the moment take on a heightened sense of purpose. While happiness sometimes calls for sacrifice and self-denial, this is all part of the flourishing that imbues our lives with meaning. The contemporary emphasis on hedonistic pleasures and short-term highs runs counter to the peaceful sense of contentment and at-one-ness with the universe that characterizes happiness in deeper traditions of thought. Perpetual happiness is not our birthright, nor will most of us achieve such a state, but over the course of a lifetime, a life lived as much for others as for oneself yields the greatest happiness overall.

Putting Selfishness Aside

Those whose actions spring from love go beyond self-interest and tap into a part of the human psyche in which selfishness is overwhelmed by concern for and attentiveness to others. The universal loving self exudes a consistent serenity and joy. A quest for ever more material things simply cannot achieve this for us.

When I finished graduate school in 1983, I took a job for two years at a college in Michigan, where my annual income was $15,000. My wife and I did not have much, and we sometimes struggled to buy baby formula and diapers for our newborn daughter. But we were happy with the very simple gifts of life, and we cultivated an attitude of gratitude. Nowadays I make a little more money, but I am no happier than I was in those simpler years. Life has become more complex and the bills are bigger, but life has not gotten measurably happier. I marvel at people like Baruch Spinoza and Walt Whitman, who were described as remarkably happy as they lived very simple lives.

Some people, overly stimulated by the drive for consumer goods, never pursue happiness beyond immediate physical gratification. This level of happiness is based on pleasure-seeking: Some external stimulus (a new car, a new outfit, a new watch) provides instant gratification, but that sense of short-term happiness does not endure. So we consume more exotic coffees, buy expensive computer games, and strive to acquire more and more things on the "hedonistic treadmill." Appreciation for simple gifts and natural wonders subsides. The bottom line: We are trapped by things that we don't even want and become more bored with life than happy. Our children may rebel against this emptiness if they hear the call of a shared humanity or sense that "things" matter more

Those who are not looking for happiness are the most likely to find it, because those who are searching forget that the surest way to be happy is to seek happiness for others.

—MARTIN LUTHER KING JR.

to their parents than does love or spirituality itself. I once coined a saying that has caught on: "It's simple to be happy but it's difficult to be simple."

A Self-Defeating Spiral
of Achievement

Other people will not grasp the happiness of contributing to the lives of others, not because they are trapped in an endless cycle of hedonism or acquisition of material things, but because they are trapped in a spiral of their own achievements, reputation, and self-promotion. These people strike me as especially unfortunate. When they enter a room for a meeting, they tout all their latest accomplishments and seem to use the word *I* incessantly. At some point, it becomes clear that advantage, power, and control over others mean everything to them. These people may even deny themselves hedonistic pleasures to enhance their personal achievement and status.

Their single-minded focus on self and ego does not result in deep happiness; in fact, it may bring on an existential crisis. Yet because their world is no bigger than themselves, fulfillment constantly eludes them.

But the ultimate happiness that infuses genuine meaning into life is the by-product of Godly love, which fills our hearts when we contribute to the lives of others, even when we feel that our natural capacities for love have waned. In Godly love we relate to others not because they contribute to our own selfish agendas (in Martin Buber's terminology, *I-It*), but because they are centers of value independent of us and equally significant to God. We approach them with awe, respect, and concern (in Buber's schema, *I-Thou*). This confers the highest form of happiness, and it is magnificent.

Love's Magnificence

It is so magnificent that we can do good in the world even though people with whom we interact may be unkind, dishonest, jealous, small-minded, cynical, and critical behind our backs. Love triumphs anyway. Never think about whether people will love you back; this concern is bound to lead to frustration. Just love and let the rest take care of itself.

It is so magnificent that we can do good in the world even when change seems unlikely, our actions seem insignificant, and people doubt our authenticity because they doubt love itself.

It is so magnificent that we can do good in the world even when we are stricken with illness, frail with old age, and at death's door. Those who frown on love can still be loved, and there is a special sort of value in this. God is love, and love will find a way. Most people

When an affluent society would coax us to believe that happiness consists in the size of our automobiles, the impressiveness of our houses, and the expensiveness of our clothes, Jesus reminds us, "A man's life consisteth not in the abundance of the things which he possesseth."

—MARTIN LUTHER KING JR.,
THE STRENGTH TO LOVE

who have been exemplars of love and have changed the world in some way small or large have encountered troubles that have been seen as nothing more than pebbles on the road.

Some of us do take paths other than love, but these paths are objectively false and always destructive of our own happiness and of those around us. We may labor under the illusion of happiness, but in the end no one will come to our funeral. Real happiness has everything to do with our capacity for concern, understanding, and sympathy; joy and humor; and an appreciation of the good and the beautiful in life. Our emotional lives must be suffused and ordered by love if we are ever to be happy.

Lord, make me an instrument of thy peace.
Where there is hatred, let me sow love;
where there is injury, pardon; where there
is doubt, faith; where there is despair,
hope; where there is sadness, joy;
where there is darkness, light.

—ST. FRANCIS OF ASSISI

8. THE WHEEL OF LOVE—
Ten Ways

 WROTE MOST OF this little meditation on "The Wheel of Love" on a late-night bus ride from Washington, D.C., to Cleveland on June 27, 2004, but it is a model about which I have written for three decades:

God, strengthen us in the different ways of love—

Forgiveness: Enable us to forgive and make our apologies meaningful;

Carefrontation: Strengthen us in the courage to confront evil in its many forms,

including injustice, with wisdom rather
than malice;

Celebration: Let us see all lives as your gifts,
calling us to thankful celebration;

Mirth: Inspire in us the warm humor and
mirthful joy that frees all from anxiety;

Loyalty: Keep us loyal, especially to those
who are shattered by life;

Respect: Give us a reverence that frees us
from the desire to manipulate others;

Listening: Humble us for attentive listening
so that others might feel valued;

Compassion: Deepen our awareness of the
suffering of others and give us the desire
to relieve it;

Helpfulness: Prompt us to lend a helping
hand to those around us;

Creativity: Help us to use our creative gifts for the good of humanity.

LOVE IS SELF-FULFILLING

All these ways of love have something in common. Whether we are listening attentively, writing a thank-you note, teaching a child to read, offering forgiveness, donating to a charity, or knitting a scarf for the needy, all these ways of love are fulfilling for us as givers. Love is not self-diminishing, but rather self-fulfilling. As Søren Kierkegaard wrote, there is nothing wrong with love of self; the problem is that we do not know how to love ourselves properly. How do we love ourselves properly? When we love God and love our neighbor as ourselves. And it is Godly love that allows us to do so, especially when loving is hard, when we enter the desert spaces, when our hearts would otherwise be darkly indifferent. The double love

We cannot really love anybody with
whom we never laugh.
—AGNES REPLIER

The only way to speak the truth is
speaking lovingly.
—HENRY DAVID THOREAU

ommandment prescribes love for God with mind and heart, and in this relationship we are given that graceful Godly love that makes it possible for us to love those we, as creatures, would otherwise disdain.

All these ways of love are ways of participating in the life of God. Loyalty, listening, and creativity, as well as all the other ways of love, are part of the very nature of God, and in these practices we can find a level of being that is resonant with God.

Creativity is one of my wife's strengths. It is amazing to see how meticulous she is in creating little gifts for the children in her preschool class. Fortunately, we can all express love through creativity, and we do not need to be famous to do so. I am, however, amazed at how super-creators like Thomas Edison used their special gifts. The cellist Pablo Casals was one of the finest musicians of his generation, and he purposely used his creative gifts to spread a message of love. Here is one of his famous quotes:

> Each person has inside a basic decency and goodness. If he listens to it and acts on it, he is giving a great deal of what the world needs most. It is not complicated, but it takes courage. It takes courage for a person to listen to his own goodness and act on it.

Casals lived a very long life, and contributed through music to the lives of millions. His "way" of love was creativity, and it is said that people who heard him perform felt the emotion of love in his music. Contrary to the notion that creativity is a form of madness, creativity at its best, is a form of love.

The Two Hardest Ways of Love

One of the two most difficult ways of love is carefrontation. There are some types of people who are able to confront others out of love. I know a gentleman whom some call the "velvet hammer" because he speaks the truth with astonishing love to those whose actions and attitudes are destructive and hurtful. The changes he brings about in difficult people are almost always extraordinary because he affirms people in love even as he helps them address their problems. But not all people exude love in this way. Other people are gifted listeners, using their gifts as counselors. Most people have several strengths, and they should nurture all of them. Godly love can inspire us to cultivate whatever strengths we have, and it can also make us stronger in areas where we do not naturally shine.

M. Scott Peck, author of the popular clas-

The children of light must be armed with the wisdom of the children of darkness but remain free of their malice.

—REINHOLD NIEBUHR, *THE CHILDREN OF LIGHT AND THE CHILDREN OF DARKNESS*

You shall not take vengeance or bear a grudge . . . but you shall love your neighbor as yourself.

—LEVITICUS 19:18

sic *The Road Less Traveled* and a graduate of psychiatry at Cast Western Reserve University's School of Medicine in the 1950s, believed "tough love" in carefrontation is an important component to love, as he communicated to me in correspondence. Scott and I became pen pals in 2002 until his passing a few years later. He wrote me a letter on April 15, 2002, that begins, "Dear Stephen, Please forgive me for using your first name, but I more than sense that we are rather kindred spirits." In the letter, he shared his views on my use of the term "unlimited love" at my institute and in my research, stating that "unlimited" love or "unconditional" love "does not seem to make much room for 'tough love' or for the times when we must focus almost entirely upon loving ourselves or for the thousands of complex decisions involved in loving well."

For a psychiatrist treating people with every kind of personality disorder, Scott naturally emphasized that love must often be firm and tough in order to be clinically successful. He went on, "Indeed, I do not think it is possible to live without limits or for that matter to love without limits." In the end, Scott suggested that I consider focusing on the term "transcendent love," meaning a divine love that alone is unlimited, although we might participate in it to degrees. While I appreciated and respected Scott's views as a psychiatrist, "unlimited" love does refer to a Godly and transcendent love, and to the ways in which we can participate in that Godly love and sometimes do amazing things with amazing grace. There is no doubt that any effective love, whether Godly or human, at times needs to be tough, set limits, and be firm in these limits. But this toughness remains a strategy of a loyal and unlimited love, a love that is unconditional at the deepest level but expressed on the surface as conditioned. Yes, we need tough love.

In this letter to me, Scott finished as follows: Among other things, I am extremely familiar with the fact that managing and directing a nonprofit organization is not at all an easy job. It almost requires unlimited love, and certainly requires transcendent love." Scott's language was always graceful and generous in his manner. One of my favorite memories of corresponding with Scott is that he wrote from "Bliss Road" in New Preston, Connecticut. With a best-seller like *The Road Less Traveled*, he deserved to live in bliss.

The second most difficult way of love is forgiveness. Forgiving others is a lot more complicated than just approaching them with outstretched arms. Our tendency to exact revenge runs deep, and even when we think we have left hurts behind, we find ourselves revisiting those feelings of resentment and bitterness again and again. Forgiveness requires us to think about all the hurts we have caused,

He became as good a friend, as good a master, and as good a man, as the good old city knew, or any other good old city, town, or borough, in the good old world. Some people laughed to see the alteration in him, but he let them laugh, and little heeded them; for he was wise enough to know that nothing ever happened on this globe, for good, at which some people did not have their fill of laughter in the outset.

—CHARLES DICKENS, *A CHRISTMAS CAROL*,
SPEAKING OF SCROOGE

to understand that it is usually hurt people who hurt others, and to sometimes think a little more deeply about the forgiving love that God has for the ones who have troubled us. To do this, it helps to relinquish to God our bitterness and desire for revenge, and let Divine love and justice handle things. It helps greatly to have a faith community in which forgiveness is modeled and exemplified, and prayed for and enacted in ritual. Forgiveness is a way of love that we all need to practice.

As far as helping and compassion are concerned, when we show up and show a heartfelt concern, our presence transmits the most important message of them all: You are significant to me and I want to be there for you. We do not need to be professionals or qualified in some special way to be present and convey this kind of emotional and healing support. Often, we just need to provide quiet companionship and keep someone company. The word

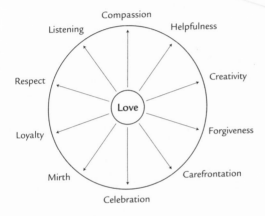

A WHEEL OF LOVE

amateur comes from the Latin word for "love," *amare*. Showing up can be brief, and often people with severe illness cannot handle anything more. Wherever you are, take the time to smile and acknowledge people, and this will spread the spirit of love far and wide.

Love can be expressed in many different ways because human needs vary greatly, and in each expression Godly love can translate our human love into something brighter, stronger, and better. None of us excel in all the ways of love, and we should build on our inherent strengths. Love is like the hub of a wheel, sending out spokes in different directions, depending on what special form or expression of love the recipient needs at the time.

If I give away all my possessions,
and if I hand over my body so that
I may boast, but do not have love,
I gain nothing.

—1 CORINTHIANS 13:3

9. Self-Sacrifice

I N March 1997 I took my daughter Emma up to New Hampshire because she was considering going to boarding school there. She had quickly decided to remain home in Shaker Heights, so we left the open house early and headed for Boston with an afternoon to ourselves. We drove into Cambridge and parked in Harvard Square. My daughter wanted to buy some jeans, and I said to her, "Emma, you go shopping. I am going to Harvard Memorial Chapel to say a prayer." I walked over to the chapel and said my prayer. I asked God to help create a dialogue between theologians and scientists on the topic of agape love, and I promised that I would be ready to make the sacrifices to nurture this process along.

I felt the presence of Godly love that afternoon, so I was not surprised when things fell into place, with the help of Sir John Templeton, for the founding of the Institute for Research on Unlimited Love (www.unlimitedloveinstitute. com) in 2001. It takes some courage, commitment, and hard work to create such an institute in an academic medical center like Case Western Reserve University's School of Medicine. Now, in addition to the Institute for Research on Unlimited Love, we have embarked on a new project at www.godlyloveproject.org to study people's spiritual experiences of Godly love.

But I do not believe in sacrifice for the sake of sacrifice. Every human being has an equal value under the canopy of Godly love, and each of us is encouraged to flourish and rejoice in the experience of this love. Godly love does not require us to nullify our own desires and aspirations, or to subsume them within this Divine love; rather, it calls on us to become one with Godly love and to share its blessings with everyone. Love of self only becomes a problem when we see ourselves as separate from the common good and act in ways that undermine and damage that common good. The goal here is not some form of self-annihilation or self-extinction, but rather for us to flourish in love and to inspire our neighbor to flourish in the same way.

Many actions mistakenly described as *self-sacrificial* only seem so because they are viewed from a wrongheaded perspective. People erroneously assert that humans are motivated solely by egoism; according to this view, living by the golden rule—Do unto others as you would have them do unto you—is much more extraordinary and demanding than it really is.

Every moment is made glorious by
the light of Love.

—RUMI, ISLAMIC SUFI MYSTIC AND POET

Self-sacrifice is the real miracle out of which
all the reported miracles grow.

—RALPH WALDO EMERSON

After all, it takes no more energy and time to be kind than it does to be nasty or cruel.

GLOBAL INTERDEPENDENCE

The flourishing of the self cannot be separated from the flourishing of others, something we all intuitively realize in our interactions with family and friends. With climate change, geo-political instability, and economic uncertainties threatening the earth as a whole, almost all of us now realize that we are only going to survive on this planet if our creative altruism encompasses all of humankind; that is, if we recognize that our own well-being is intricately intertwined with everyone else's. Godly love rejects the dualism between self and other, between egoism and altruism, that has characterized so much of Western thought. Rather than condemning individuals for seeking happiness, I consider happiness to be the highest good. Those who frame their lives around genuine love for others understand that, as a byproduct or indirect effect of such wide-ranging compassion, they will flourish emotionally, and, in the context of any healthy community, they will flourish socially as well.

But there are times in life when we must give in ways that are extremely demanding, even overwhelming. The giver may feel stressed or pressured, inner harmony and flourishing falling by the wayside, if too much is asked or required of the self in devotion to others or to a noble cause. In these deserts, these periods of desolation and soul-sapping stress, spirituality and the energy of Godly love become especially crucial. Sometimes we must draw boundaries in life so that we can go into retreat and restore our energy and purpose. When circumstances preclude this, self-discipline, pacing, and the spirituality of Godly love become even more important. Sometimes there is just not enough respite for the caregiver of a loved one with a chronic illness, and giving really does begin to take a toll. Suffering becomes very real; then we must dig deep into the spiritual well of Godly love so as not to become bitter and angry.

Noble Sacrifices

Some theologians scoff at the link between Godly love and flourishing by pointing out a long list of martyrs. But these martyrs were violating the spirit of Godly love if they were seeking their demise in some deliberate, and therefore masochistic, way. On the other hand, people such as Bonhoeffer or Martin Luther King Jr. were true martyrs because they were not looking for the Cross, but it seemed to be looking for them, and they accepted it with courage as part of God's calling. In such cases, sacrifice is noble and good, even to the end.

Greater love hath no man than this, that he
lay down his life for his friends.

—JOHN 15:13

Bonhoeffer had won over the hearts of his Nazi prison guards to such an extent that they were deeply saddened when the order arrived from Hitler for the pastor's execution.

Despite all I have written about love and flourishing, I worry about a culture in which hedonism, individualism, and the materialism leave no room for the genuine sacrifice that love sometimes requires. Talk of self-realization and self-actualization can blind us to the fact that on some occasions in most of our lives, we must love to the point where our own desires are subsumed by another's needs. Sometimes deep commitments require considerable or even extreme self-sacrifice. Here Godly love can sustain a sense of inner joy, even if the Cross that we do not seek happens to find us.

I began this book with an allusion to Isaiah 35:1, the desert and the rose, and asserted that

It is a far, far better thing that I do, than
I have ever done; it is a far, far better rest
that I go to, than I have ever known.
—SYDNEY CARTON, IN CHARLES DICKENS'
A TALE OF TWO CITIES

Godly love can empower us to triumph over adversity, even when life disappoints us greatly, or harshness surrounds us, or the sacrifices demanded of us seem too onerous to bear. In such times we can still experience Godly love, and from this come faith, hope, love, gratitude, forgiveness, and joy. We can, if need be, sacrifice ourselves fully in nobility and love.

God is love, and those who abide
in love abide in God, and God
abides in them.

—2 JOHN 4:16

10. A Useful Exercise—

Godly Love Prayer, Visualization, and Action

W HEN I RISE in the morning, which is usually quite early before people have had a chance to intrude on the quietness, I pray a bit for the gift of Godly love, and then I take a while, with eyes closed but imagination open, to visualize the interactions to come during the course of the day. I usually know my schedule, so I visualize each interaction, from those with my wife and children to those with the many people I will be meeting that day, from the groups to whom I may be speaking, to the individuals scheduled for a conference call. I ask myself, one by one, how can that person or those peo-

And now faith, hope, and love abide, these
three: and the greatest of these is love.

—1 CORINTHIANS 3:13

le best be loved? What does my heart and what does Godly love want me to give them? Some people need compassion, some a little confrontation, others an expression of loyalty or perhaps celebration. By very briefly visualizing these interactions I set the stage for the day before it really begins. I gain a sense of genuine intentionality—"I am living today to express the ways of love, and to draw on Godly love in every interaction without exception." I ask God to help me in this endeavor to spread love in small ways throughout the course of the day. Godly love becomes my partner for the day. And then I try to act accordingly, to make these loving intentions and rehearsed interactions become reality. They usually do. Actions are key; otherwise this is a purely internal exercise of no great value or purpose.

When I fail to pray and visualize, as can occur on a very busy morning when I have to rush to get my morning routine completed on

time, the day never goes as well. My interac
tions have less purpose and intentional focus
and I never feel as fulfilled as I would like.

Infusing Each Day with Godly Love

So always put love and Godly love at the cente
of your life, and have confidence that no time o
situation is so challenging that Godly love can
not enter your life and show you the way. If we
pay attention to Godly love, our lives are infi
nitely happier and healthier than they woul
be otherwise. Sometimes I say or do the wrong
thing, of course, but people do not remembe
these things for long. What they remember i
how I made them feel like human beings o
significance and dignity under the protective
umbrella of Godly love.

There is so much freedom in a life of love. I
is freedom from the prison of self that eventu

lly leaves us isolated, unfulfilled, and even ill. We may not let on that we are as empty and unhappy as we are, and for months, even years, we may give the proud appearance of prosperity and self-fulfillment. But with our last breath, as our life passes before us, we will know that all was in vain and know that it is better not to live than not to love.

We must think of God as one who listens to us and is close to us in times of greatest need, no matter what we have suffered. It is wrong to blame God for things that go wrong in life. No one gets out of life alive, and we are frail creatures, gone from the earth in a flash of geologic time. Place your suffering in the category of mystery. When tragedy strikes, as it inevitably will, thank God for being available and present as a comforting energy that enables you to be resilient. Do not think of God as the cause of misery. We need to think of God instead as the Ultimate Love that is always there with open

But I always think that the best way to know
God is to love many things.
—VINCENT VAN GOGH

Where you find no love, put love,
and you will find love.
—JOHN OF THE CROSS

We make a living by what we get,
we make a life by what we give.
—WINSTON CHURCHILL